# The Power of the Goddess

## A Woman's Journey to Awakening, Cultivating, and Sustaining Her Power

# The Power of the Goddess

A Woman's Journey
to Awakening, Cultivating, and
Sustaining Her Power

By Marjean Holden

LEON SMITH
PUBLISHING

www.LeonSmithPublishing.com

# *Dedication*

This book is dedicated to each and every person who has ever gone through the pain of low self-esteem, stress-related disorders, anxiety, burnout, or exhaustion. I empathize with you and bless you with abundant health and wellness.

# Acknowledgments

I would like to acknowledge from the depths of my heart the following:

First, thank Goddess. Thank Goddess or God or Universe—whatever you might call the Creator of all—for bringing me to this time and place right here, right now.

I thank my parents, Diana and Oscar Holden: You never put a cap on the things that I could accomplish, even when what I was talking about didn't make sense to you. You were always in full support. Thank you for your love and guidance. Thank you for what you taught me and also for helping me seek and find answers on my own. I love you. Pops—I miss you tremendously and know you watch over all of us every day.

My sister, Lisa, and brother, Kevin: I could not have asked for two better siblings in this lifetime to play with. You are both giant wells of inspiration for me and always have been. Thank you for all the crap you gave me growing up as your little sister—and for all the love you have given me so freely. I love you.

My ancestors, who came before me to pave the way: You are my non-physical team that spurs me on and clears my paths. I am eternally grateful for your light and all of the adversity that you endured before transitioning to the spirit world.

My sistahs: Jennifer Steed, Cheri Atchison, Christiana Carter, and Juliana Kramer. You are the Goddesses who held me, encouraged me, loved me, listened to me, guided me, laughed with me, cried with me, and who were so supportive of me when I was in my deepest, darkest, most painful places. There is no amount of love and gratitude that I can verbally express to you all for the impact you had on my life in those dark moments. My heart and soul are eternally grateful, and I love you all so very much.

Thanks also to Nicole Daedone, Rachel Cherwitz, Aubrey Anne Fuller, Marcus Rathnathican, Robert Kendall, and Andreas Panosian—my Orgasmic Meditation teachers, mentors, and friends. Meeting all of you in my most depleted state was such a gift, and one of the most important turning points of my life. Simply Magic. Namaste and NAM MYOHO RENGE KYO!

Keith and Maura Leon: A very special thanks to both of you. You have been such a positive, powerful influence in my life since the day I met you. Thank you for honoring me, inspiring me, and giving me some attention and love when I needed it most. You have always been encouraging and supportive of me in my efforts to share my gifts with others. You have created a space for me to make my thoughts cohesive, so I could express them to the world. There are no words to adequately express my gratitude to you. Thank you both from the depths of my heart and soul. May our kinship be eternally blessed and surrounded by the abundance of God's love and light.

# Contents

# *Introduction*

Hello! This book is about you. It's about the power that is inside of you.

You may not know that power yet, but it is there. You may already have some sense of it, but haven't had the opportunity, the tools, the information, or the self-discovery to access it, cultivate it, and make use of it in your life.

That is what this book is all about—finding the power that is within you, so that you can shine it out to the world.

I am writing this book after having been to a place where I felt absolutely powerless. I didn't know which way to turn, and I couldn't find helpful resources. I struggled through it and gained some insights from my struggles. I am hopeful that what I learned can help you on your journey.

I was a strong, independent woman in charge of my life. My life was filled with successes and accomplishments and constant movement, but eventually I found myself in a position where I couldn't even move to get out of bed. Finally I was able to bring myself back to a place where I actually felt good. It was a difficult journey.

I made some discoveries along the way about the dynamics of feminine power. I hope that writing my story can help other people who are struggling.

Harnessing feminine power—for both women and men—can be key to creating a balanced life. Learning to understand your feminine energy is vital. Whether you are a man or a woman, putting that energy into balance with your masculine energy can be a difficult task. When you can cultivate this balance, it will enable you to manage your life, meet your goals, and have a peaceful, happy existence.

Read this book with an open mind and a clean slate. Whether you are in crisis or are trying to learn more about your feminine power, open your mind. Whether you're in inspiration mode or in desperation mode, be open. Take your time. You don't have to rush through it. Really absorb it. Let it sink in.

When you find something that resonates with you, keep it.

If something doesn't resonate with you, let it go.

When I read books, I don't expect every word to be meaningful to me. It may be the last chapter, or the last sentence that truly speaks to me. Look for the things that resonate with you, that feel right for you in this moment. Your consciousness is not going to be able to understand or pick up anything else.

Maybe you will read the book a number of times and will pick up different things each time. Some books I have read over and over again and have picked up something different every single time because I was a different person each time I read the book. So give yourself the opportunity to be open, take what works for you, use those things, and come back to everything else later.

My desire is that you understand more about yourself after reading this book. I hope to help you understand that there is a great power inside of you that is waiting to come out and shine into the world. I hope that you find little spots in yourself that may not look like much at first glance, but are amazing nuggets of gold to be worked with. You are full of little lumps of coal ready to be shaped into diamonds.

I hope that you find a sense of your own unique power and gain new tools, ideas, and guidelines for setting yourself up for success.

Above all, I hope that you become able to accept and appreciate yourself for all that you are, for every single beautiful cell and every part of you that exists.

I hope that you find peace and a deep understanding that no matter where you are, you are not alone.

# CHAPTER ONE

# Awakening the Goddess

## ACCEPTING YOURSELF AS A WOMAN

Acceptance is one of the keys to freedom in your life — from accepting what is happening in the moment to accepting what is going on in your life to accepting who you are.

Acceptance doesn't mean always saying, "Oh, isn't this the greatest thing ever?!"

Perhaps something is going on at the moment that is not so great. However, only when you are able to accept it can you move on beyond what is happening. Once you accept what is happening, you can go forward in spite of obstacles. You can move into a place where you can begin to take action.

Accepting yourself as a woman — for the women who are reading this — is key to moving forward and owning your power as a woman. In this day and age, this power is very different in our society than you might believe. The world has changed and is continuing to change.

For many years, I struggled with accepting myself as a woman. Initially, I didn't think it was going to be a big deal, but it turned out to be a tougher process than I had anticipated.

From childhood, I had always possessed this mindset: *If a boy can do it, I can do it.*

In fact, I usually thought: *If a boy can do it, I can do it — better!*

It was true sometimes, but it was not always the best and healthiest way to approach my goals.

## The Class Tomboy

I'm going to take you back to when I was young. I grew up having a deep sense that my dad wanted me to be a boy.

I don't know why I had this sense. Maybe it was because my dad would wrestle with me and do things a father would typically do with his son. I did have a brother. But I always had this sense as we went fishing and played sports together that my dad really wanted me to be a boy.

As a result, I was the classic tomboy. I became good at all the sports I tried. I was an all-around athlete. From a very early age, I focused exclusively on these active skills.

I was Daddy's little girl, but I was always Daddy's little tomboy-girl.

In my mind, success was all about what I could do with my body. It took many years, until I was well into my thirties, to understand that my power lay not so much in what I could *do*; rather, it was in the grace and finesse of the feminine power inside me.

It is actually this feminine power that has enabled me to maneuver through the biggest obstacles and challenges of my life.

Ever the tomboy, I didn't have any dates in high school. I was the jock, I was the superstar, and I was everybody's buddy. I was every guy's buddy, but never a girlfriend. I didn't get a sense of being in a woman's body until I was in college and started attracting attention from guys in a different way.

Are you a tomboy?

If you are, know that there is another side to you. There is a woman in there who wants to come out.

## Becoming a Strong, Independent Woman Requires Vulnerability

"I can do it all myself. I don't need anyone else."

Does that sound familiar?

In society today, women are conditioned to be strong and independent. We are supposed to be able to do it all ourselves; we don't need anybody for anything. We certainly don't need to rely on a man. I went down this road for many years, and I can tell you that this perspective can be limiting.

Are you like this?

There is nothing wrong with being a strong, independent woman; it has many benefits.

But do you leave room for anyone else to offer you their gifts?

Do you ever allow someone to help you out when you are struggling?

Do you ever let a man buy you a meal?

Do you feel like you *owe* somebody if they do anything nice for you?

Are you uncomfortable with leaning on anyone?

Many of us who have been raised to be strong, independent women have trouble with vulnerability. We have been taught to be uncomfortable with what we perceive as weakness. Allowing yourself to lean on someone else is acknowledging your vulnerability.

Although it may not feel like it, being able to accept your vulnerability is not a weakness at all. It is actually a strength.

We are human, and we all need other people in this lifetime. If your fear of being vulnerable is keeping you from getting close to other people—your life is incomplete, although you may not know it.

To truly be a strong, independent woman, you must allow yourself to be open and vulnerable at times. You must be able to ask for the things you want and need.

## Laying Down the Sword

What I'm about to say may be extremely challenging for some of you.

How do I know this?

I know it from experience, of course—because it was extremely challenging for me.

Are you a battler?

Are you always fighting for your beliefs and to attain your goals?

Although this might feel scary and unnatural, you need to lay down your sword and stop fighting.

For years, I was fighting constantly. I was fighting to defend myself, fighting to be the best I could, and fighting to achieve—I got to a point where I was exhausted. I was so tired of being my own knight in shining armor; I was wielding my sword all the time. It was chopping down trees, it was cutting through challenges; my sword was never resting. Eventually, I was exhausted.

I was lying in bed, not able to move or get up, and a Spirit said to me: *It's time to lay down your sword.*

And—oh my gosh—this is something that resonated with me immediately. Listening to this voice changed my world.

*Lay down your sword.*

The sword can come back out again from time to time. But laying down the sword, not being your own knight in shining armor all the time, is critical.

Always being combative leads to burnout, stress, and anxiety—results that are not much fun, speaking from personal experience.

I also remember hearing this same advice from my mentor, Alison Armstrong, about relationships with men. She counseled that if you lay down your sword, it is easier to look for the good in your partner.

Laying down the sword is an act of kindness toward yourself. Allow yourself to be in the mindset that even as a strong, independent woman, you don't always have to have your sword at the ready.

Relax and breathe.

## APPROVING OF YOURSELF AS A WOMAN

Part of my difficulty in accepting myself as a woman centered on approval issues.

I was driven by my father's approval of my athletic pursuits as a child but had trouble finding approval of myself as a woman. I remember, when I was young, being upset that I was a woman and not a man. I saw men get things that women were not allowed to have. I saw it in the workplace, in sports, and other parts of society.

For me, life was challenging until I realized the power I had in being a woman. But I didn't know how to access this power.

I didn't have anyone to teach me what being a woman was about. Even though my mom was around, we didn't share those kinds of conversations. We weren't an openly communicative family. Eventually, I had to seek out other women to find answers.

I didn't like many elements of womanhood. It took a long time to feel good about my cycles. I didn't feel comfortable with my emotions.

In my early twenties, I was told by a boyfriend to stop crying because it was weak.

There was a long period of time after that in which I didn't show any emotion.

## Underlying Beliefs About Yourself

My underlying belief growing up was that it wasn't okay to be a woman.

I thought:

- *It isn't okay to act like a girl.*
- *It isn't okay to be strong in a feminine way, only in a masculine way.*
- *It isn't okay to be emotional.*
- *It is certainly not okay to cry.*

I thought it was not okay to have any of the behaviors that are naturally inherent to being a girl and as a result, I resisted these natural behaviors.

I once met a very wise woman. Her name is Luisah Teish, and she is a *Mother*, or priestess, in one of the African-culture religions called *Ifa*.

Once, when doing a divination reading for me, she said, "You have a problem with being a woman."

I didn't understand what she meant.

She said, "The divinations don't lie. They say there is something you need to work on as far as approving of yourself as a woman and that you are a woman in this lifetime."

She was right. It was hard to approve of myself as a woman—that I was emotional, vulnerable, needed help every once in a while, and to approve of myself being considered girly in any way.

I came to realize that I had a difficult time embracing my womanhood in this lifetime because of some past-life energies that I carried with me.

From the Dark Ages to the early 1900s, every time period has possessed stigmas for women and restrictions on their behavior. I carried these past-life energies with me; issues I needed to clean up on a karmic level. I had to overcome these burdens in order to approve of myself in the here and now, in this lifetime as a woman. It was a hard road for me.

Once I had accepted my womanhood and began to appreciate these elements of myself, my life started to smooth out a bit. But it did take me quite a long time to get to that point.

What are your underlying beliefs about women?

If you are a woman, what are your underlying beliefs about yourself?

I advise you to accept that you are a woman, no matter your age. There are certain feminine behaviors that come along with that. Accept and approve of all of them, for yourself and for the women around you.

## Women Who Use Their Femininity to Manipulate

Part of the reason I was not happy to be a woman was due to what I saw growing up. I grew up in an affluent neighborhood. I witnessed many unpleasant examples of behavior in the women around me. I saw women act in an overtly manipulative fashion in order to get what they wanted. I saw women putting on acts instead of being genuine.

In particular, I saw many examples of women acting purposely weak.

This kind of behavior always bothered me immensely.

So I thought: *I won't ever be that way. I'll go the other way. I will be strong and independent, and I won't need anybody. I won't be indebted to anybody.*

I could never understand those women who would use their sexuality, their femininity, or their beauty, in order to manipulate situations to their benefit. As an actress in Hollywood for many years, I saw a great deal of this. Many times, I saw women using men for their money or power, and it was sickening to me.

This behavior irritated the deepest part of my being and my soul; to manipulate by using the feminine felt so wrong. It didn't feel attractive. It felt like an ugly thing to me, and there was no way I was going to be like that.

As a young woman, I often sat in judgment of other women when I saw them manipulate. Sometimes I judged harshly without knowing all of the facts, when I didn't know the woman, the situation, her education, or her background.

It took some experience to understand that there is always a story behind everything.

I didn't have the insight back then to be able to say to myself: *Maybe this person has never had anyone to teach her to be any different.*

After my grandfather died, I remember being shocked that my grandmother didn't know how to balance a checkbook. I didn't like that she lacked that ability. But she never learned how; it was a big lesson for me about judging people.

## Being a Woman Isn't So Bad After All

Yep—huge breakthrough for me! Once I really got that—I mean *really* got that, really settled into accepting that I am a woman in this lifetime—I could actually start to heal those places that needed healing. Being a woman was actually pretty cool!

Of course, this realization didn't happen overnight, but once I started embracing the fact of the matter, I could take it one step at a time. Which, in reality, is the *only* way to get anything done: one step at a time. I started to search, to seek ways in which I could embrace being a woman. I searched for mentors, courses, books, anything that was going to help me to understand more of myself, more of my core essence, more of how to truly accept myself at a fundamental level.

Now, when I look back, I think: *I really had some deeply rooted beliefs that it is not okay to be a woman.*

That was hard to face. But over time, it became easier and easier. I started trusting myself, the process, and trusting that as a woman, I could really make a difference in this world. I began to trust that through my journey, I could shed light into the places that needed it most. I could shine light into my own darkness that in turn, may help someone else down the road come into more of themselves.

Once I became a mom, well, that was the life experience that sealed the deal for me. I got to reflect on all the things I would have liked to have been told and guided on while I was growing up. Now, I get to heal a lot of my own pain through guiding my daughter on her path. Now *that* is really cool.

I get to help shape and mold my daughter and give her tools that I didn't have. I get to be there for her to discuss all things feminine. *Everything.*

It isn't always easy; sometimes the explanations take some creative thinking on my part, but it is so worth it.

## KNOWING THAT IT'S SAFE TO BE A WOMAN

Just as I had not accepted and approved of being a woman, I haven't always felt safe being a woman.

Personally, I believe strongly in past lives and other lifetimes. I am sensitive to energies from other time periods in which I've lived. My sense of safety is not only a reflection of my current life, but of my past lives, in which there were many challenges for me as a woman.

In this lifetime, I have trained myself to be physically, mentally, and emotionally strong, but there are other elements of safety for me. Fearing disapproval, I have often not felt safe expressing myself as a woman.

I will do what it takes in order to accomplish the goals, dreams, desires, and purpose of my life. But along the way, there has always been the fear that I'd either be called a ballbuster or a bitch — or some other derogatory word for a woman who knows what she wants and isn't afraid to go after it.

Feeling safe comes from developing your internal power. Cultivating self-approval, establishing boundaries, and finding your voice are all important elements of this process.

## Seeking the Approval of Others

Do you seek the approval of others?

We all want to be approved of and accepted by others. As you walk through life, however, this can't be your driving force.

We can't control the actions of others. Either they accept us and approve of us, or they don't. If we base every ounce of our self-esteem and self-confidence on what other people think of us, we will be stuck in the mud forever.

Look instead for self-approval. Look at yourself and your actions critically.

Do you approve of yourself?

If you can find this kind of approval — *self*-approval — then yes, you can care about what other people think and what other people feel about you, but you won't be prevented from accomplishing a task because somebody else doesn't approve.

Having self-approval is powerful. Not requiring external approval is freeing.

Freedom is vital. Self-approval provides me with an essential form of freedom.

If you root your self-esteem and self-confidence in seeking approval from others, you will crash and burn should that approval be taken away. It will be hard to pick yourself up off the pavement and keep going with bloodied knees and bruises.

If you have self-approval, your knees might be skinned up and bleeding a little bit, but you will be able to stand up and keep moving.

If you are stuck waiting for someone else's approval, you may lie on that pavement for a very long time.

## Set Healthy Boundaries

Boundaries are vital for healthy relationships.

I was in my late forties when I learned this important fact.

Here is some of what I learned:

- Boundaries are healthy, whether it's setting a boundary with your words, your energy, or your actions.

- Boundaries are required to build your power and your confidence.

- You need to set boundaries to keep people from taking advantage of you.

- Boundaries allow you the freedom to choose your own path, to have the freedom to make the best choices for your life.

How do you set boundaries if you aren't already a confident person?

As with anything else that is new — it might be easier said than done. It's like riding a bike; you have to put the training wheels on first in order to gain your balance and confidence. Once you've done that, you take the training wheels off.

It will take practice.

We are human, and because we are human there will always be little fears that may pop up when change is happening.

You might have fearful thoughts:

> *If I say no, are they still going to like me?*
> *If I stand my ground, are they still going to approve of me?*

It took me a long time to establish boundaries, but once I started doing it, my world began to open up in ways that were absolutely amazing.

When you set healthy boundaries for yourself, you will start gaining more respect from others. We teach people how to treat us. If you don't have any boundaries, people *will* walk all over you because you are letting them.

I had a situation in which this person would call me and dump all of her negative feelings on my doorstep. At the end of our conversation, she would feel better, but I would end up feeling terrible. Her negative words and energy were dumped all over me. It happened over and over.

One day, she called, and I said, "Please stop. If you're going to dump your crap, I don't want to hear it because I end up feeling like crap. That's the end of it."

And she never did it again. We have a really great relationship now because she knows she can't do that to me.

Setting boundaries is healthy.

## You Can Have a Voice

Over the ages, it hasn't always been safe to be a woman, to speak up, to have a voice. We have evolved so much as a species. At this point in time—more than ever before—women can have a voice. Speaking up and speaking your truth is safe for the most part, and it is a powerful force for a woman to wield.

How do you find your voice?

How do you use your voice?

This is an exciting part of your journey toward the power of the feminine!

Here are some truths that I have discovered:

- You have a gift inside that wants to get out.

- Your voice is the expression of that gift.

- Don't take the term *voice* literally—you don't have to be a singer, public speaker, or writer.

- Your voice is your message, no matter who you are.

- It is your unique gift to give.

- The more you resist speaking your message, the harder your path will be.

- There will always be some people who may not like what you have to say, but you can't let that keep you silent.

- Setting your own boundaries and keeping your energy clean and clear will help you find your voice.

- Like everything else, using your voice takes practice.

Don't be afraid to have a voice and speak your truth. Whatever is inside of you that wants to speak up needs you to let it out. The more you smash and cram it down, trying to keep it inside of you, the more it will try to escape.

Find your voice. Work on yourself to strengthen your voice. Whatever it is you want to say in the world will ultimately benefit other people because your gifts are for them.

Our gifts are given to us from God, and using our gifts to help others are the gifts we give God. You have a voice. Use it.

Let your woman shine.

# CHAPTER TWO

# Accessing and Cultivating Your Power

**WHERE DOES YOUR POWER COME FROM?**

Growing up, I had many misconceptions about where my power actually came from. I thought it was exclusively in my ability to do, do, do. I was wrong.

It took a long time to understand that power is complex and involves many elements. There wasn't any one thing that released my power. It was a series of different self-discovery experiences.

Where does power come from?

We will discuss these important power factors in this section:

- Self-awareness
- Self-trust
- Self-confidence
- Self-esteem

## Self-Awareness

Without self-awareness, you will never understand where your power is coming from.

Self-awareness is being able to look at your whole self, to be able to see the parts of you that maybe aren't so pretty, as well as the parts that are admirable about you.

You must acknowledge, accept, and understand yourself in order to become self-aware. You must take a good look at all the different aspects of yourself that shape who you are to the outside world.

We dread exposing our negative personality traits to the world, and sometimes we hide them from ourselves as well.

It's a survival mechanism; it's the way that we've been taught to be in order to survive in society. Our primal brain is only set up for survival, and anything beyond that in the unknown is labeled as dangerous, scary, or painful. The definition of fear is the anticipation of pain.

You might worry about what will be revealed if you look closely at yourself.

You might be wondering:

*What if my hidden self is ugly or weak?*
*What if I am unacceptable?*

It is scary, but you must be willing to take off all of your masks to reveal your whole self in order to release your power.

Self-awareness takes courage.

## Self-Trust

Trust is difficult for many people. When we put our trust in something or someone and the result isn't what we want it to be, we are disappointed. Trusting yourself can be just as difficult.

Know that deep down inside, there is a master in all of us. Know that there is a place inside — an all-knowing, all-encompassing center, an all-powerful being — deep down at the core of yourself.

Self-trust is vital to accessing your power. If you don't trust yourself, you will never be able to believe in yourself enough to wield your own forces.

Do you have difficulty trusting yourself?

Here are some thoughts to consider:

- You need to access the deepest part of yourself and put your trust there.

- Your inner being is connected to the power of the Universe.

- Believe that whatever you need is going to be there when you need it.

- Trust that you can ask for help and you won't be criticized.

- Put more emphasis on trusting what feels right for you and what you desire.

- Your desire for yourself is directly related to your power.

- Standing up for your own values is an important step toward self-trust.

- Trusting yourself will take practice.

If you are focused on approval from other people, self-trust will be especially challenging for you. Standing up for your own values is key, and it leads to owning your power.

Trust yourself. If you need assistance with this, find someone who can give you some guidance—a life coach, a mentor, or a confidant can help you forge trust in yourself.

## Self-Esteem and Self-Confidence

When you develop this self-trust and approval of yourself, you will naturally boost your self-esteem and self-confidence. This is part of your power. Your self-esteem and self-confidence are big factors in being able to own your power.

Here are some factors to keep in mind:

- Self-confidence is built by experience.

- To build self-confidence, you need to try new things.

- When you try something new and are lacking confidence, give yourself time.

- Be willing to try again if you don't succeed the first time.

- Be patient. Impatience only results in loss of hope and giving up.

- Self-esteem is related to the way you value your internal self.

- Self-esteem is intimately tied into your self-awareness, self-trust and self-confidence.

If you find yourself in a position where your self-esteem is low, dig into it and find out why you are feeling insecure. Ask yourself questions. Get curious. Don't shame yourself for feeling the way you do. Instead, be curious about why you are feeling that way.

Your power comes from within, so it is already part of you, regardless of what presence is around you on the outside. It is woven into your inner self. Therefore, the way to access it is through the deepest elements of your mind and heart: your self-awareness, self-trust, self-confidence, and self-esteem.

## SEXUALITY AND SENSUALITY

Unless you are from a very open environment, sexuality and sensuality are subjects that aren't typically discussed. As you were growing up, you probably were not taught to cultivate your sensuality or to honor your sexuality.

So let's spend some time discussing it here.

Sensuality is a positive force. It is a powerful and creative energy and can be a wonderful part of your life.

## Don't Be Afraid of It!

For a long time, I had this idea that my sexuality had to be in the closet.

I wondered:

> *I want to have sex, but is it right?*
> *Am I bad for wanting it?*
> *Is it bad to have an appetite?*

I want to emphasize that sexuality is natural. We are human beings, and we are animals. We are a species of animals. Every single animal procreates. Every single person has a sexual energy. We've all come from a sexual process; we are all products of sexual energy.

It is too common to be shamed for your desire to have sex, especially if you are a woman. But remember, your power comes from your desire. If you have a sexual desire and you've been taught that it's bad or wrong, you are going to repress it. This will result in the suppression of your power.

It took a long time, until I was in my late forties, to learn that having a sexual appetite isn't wrong. It is healthy. It is freeing.

Moreover, once you can accept your innate sexuality, you will free other parts of you that have desires, and open up new sources of power.

## Explore Your Sexuality

Explore your sexuality. Whenever you feel yourself discrediting or discounting your feelings, stop and open up instead. Don't be afraid. Maybe you are a bit more sexual or sensual than you have been allowing yourself to be.

Here are some ideas that may help:

- You are a unique sexual being.

- Find your own safe ways of exploring your sexuality.

- If this is an uncomfortable topic for you, start slowly.

- Consider what makes you feel relaxed and open.

- Consider what gives you that warm, buttery feeling.

- Enjoy physical sensations such as a beautiful, flowing dress or scarf.

- Take a luxurious warm bath to spark sensual feelings.

I invite you to explore yourself, especially if you have never allowed yourself to be a sensual being. Shift your perception. Allow yourself to be in approval of being sexual, being sensual, by exploring this inner part of yourself.

As you start to expand and develop these natural tendencies, your relationships may be impacted as well. If you are worrying that people around you won't accept you, ask the Universe to bring people into your life that do support it.

## Own Your Sexuality

When you start to own your sexuality and sensuality, something happens. It's like a magical portal into a different dimension. It is hard to describe, but it is an extraordinary feeling to be comfortable in your own body.

But for so many years, I didn't own my sexuality. When I started to own my sexuality and approve of my own sex, I felt so much more grounded, centered, and able to handle and speak about things I needed, desired, and wanted.

Owning my sexuality has increased my capacity to set my boundaries and build my self-trust, self-confidence, and self-esteem.

Owning my power through my sexuality has enhanced every area of my life. My communication improved. I'm more grounded in all the areas of my life.

## TAPPING INTO YOUR CREATIVE POWER

Creative expression equals freedom.

You must learn to be able to express yourself in whatever way is natural for you.

You can express yourself as an artist or musician, but also as an accountant, a lawyer, or a teacher. It doesn't matter. When I say creative, I'm not saying you have to paint, make music, or dance.

I'm talking about your creative expression. There is something inside you that wants to come out. You may already know what it is and need only to gain the freedom to let it out. Or you may still need to figure out what you need to express.

### Allow Creativity to Flow

Don't be scared of the word *creativity*. Don't get fixated on your lack of artistic talent. We aren't talking about being an artist. We are all creative beings, even those of us who can't draw a straight line or sing a note on key.

Of course, artists are creative. But someone who works in computer technology is also creative. A plumber can be creative as well.

Jump in and say out loud, "I am creative."

Creativity means you are moving something from the invisible to the visible or taking what's inside of you and expressing it in the outward realm.

How do you find your own unique creative expression?

Here are some questions that may help you:

- What lights you up?
- What gives you joy?
- What makes you feel like your juices are flowing?
- What do you love to do when you're all by yourself?
- What do you love to share with other people: movement, nature, coffee?
- What is it that turns you on and sparks you inside?

Once you have some ideas, get out there and explore. Discover again what makes you feel good.

Does dancing make you feel good?

Go dance.

Does walking in the woods make you feel good?

Do that.

Does playing with a dog make you feel good?

Play away.

Does taking a bath make you feel good?

Go ahead.

Does helping someone else organize their house feel good to you?

Do it.

Do the things that make you feel good. When you feel good, whatever is inside of you is going to come out. As you explore, be observant. You are likely to find that you are naturally expressing yourself in a unique way — you are being creative.

It's different for everyone. One person's access to their creative power is going to be different than another person's access to their creative power.

Keep asking questions and take action on the things you discover. Be curious about yourself.

Remember, it is a process of self-discovery. Enjoy it, and have fun with it.

**Bringing in an Element of Fun**

When was the last time you had fun?

Seriously. Honestly.

When was the last time you had that deep, belly-rolling laugh?

When was the last time you thought: *Oh my God, that was so much fun!*

If you can't remember, it is time to find yourself some fun.

When we stop being kids and become adults, we have to be responsible. It doesn't feel important to have fun anymore. It may even feel wrong, but it isn't. In fact, it is necessary.

What is fun for you?

One of the things I like to do to maintain my sense of fun is go to the arcade and play video games because I like games. I also enjoy board games, card games, and puzzles.

Find what you like and make time for fun in your life.

## Connecting to Your Happy Inner Child

It is vital to tap in and connect to your inner child. Take yourself back to the time when you were a child and carefree. Your inner child still wants to have fun and a good time. If you don't honor that place in you that is carefree, fun, and wanting to have a good time, that part is going to get cranky and throw a tantrum.

Does it feel like these kinds of activities are a waste of time?

It might feel that way in a busy life, but don't be fooled.

Finding time for carefree fun will actually help you to achieve your adult goals. It will increase your productivity in the long run.

You have to nurture that inner being, that little kid inside of you.

Does your inner child want to have an ice cream?

Mine always wants to have ice cream, which is tough because as an adult, we don't burn the ice cream calories the way we did as a child. But sometimes, you should allow your inner child to have some fun. Give it some ice cream, take it to the park, and swing on a swing.

Sometimes you can see this need more clearly in other people around you. One of my girlfriends was denying her inner child, and I could see it was affecting her life.

I asked her what her inner child wanted to do and she told me she wanted to go to the beach to play in the sand and swim in the ocean.

I told her I would go with her and support her — and her inner child — and we did. It was a wonderful day and, boy, her inner child was so happy. It was amazing.

You will be amazed at how relaxing a short trip with your inner child can be. Sometimes, you don't even know how tense and stressed you are until the moment you are able to relax.

Honor and nurture your inner child. This is another key element of owning your power and gaining your self-confidence, self-esteem, and self-trust. When our inner child can trust us to do the things that feel good and bring that fun factor into our lives, then things will start to flow freely.

# CHAPTER THREE

# Honoring the Masculine

## WE ALL HAVE A MASCULINE SIDE

We come into the world as a particular gender. Sometimes we get mixed up and confused, and there is a different spirit inside of us than is represented in the physical form. I won't explore that because it is not my area of expertise.

We need to embrace that we are both a masculine and a feminine being. No matter what gender you are physically, we have both aspects. They are aspects of the greater whole.

We are all holistic beings who are balancing many elements; we are feminine and we are masculine, we are light and we are dark, left and right, up and down.

Embracing the components of both masculine and feminine is part of the journey to integration. On the path to wholeness, we often look for someone of the opposite sex to complete us as opposed to being complete within ourselves.

In this chapter, we will be talking about becoming complete within ourselves in both energies: masculine and feminine — whether you are a man or a woman.

## The Doer Within

The doer is the part within all of us that takes action. If you have done any sort of studying about masculine and feminine forces, you know that the part of us that takes action is usually considered the masculine. It possesses the energy of a warrior.

In our world, the doer is highly regarded. Our societies are focused on creating and attaining objects and goals. Everybody wants something and striving to attain goals is honored in our culture.

The doer is that part of us that actually takes the steps in order to be able to accomplish the thing that we seek. If you have a goal, if you want to achieve something big and grand, the masculine side of you, the doer, is going to take over. The doer will push forward and work toward the goal, breaking down any barriers along the way.

It's like being a hunter out in the forest and getting ready to bring home food for the tribe. The doer, the masculine force, will be out there with his bow and arrow, hunting the deer in an effort to bring home food.

## Honor Your Masculine Side

If you are a feminine woman, you may overlook the importance of honoring the masculine. Please don't fall into the trap of thinking you need a man, or an external masculine force, in your life to do everything for you.

If you rely on an external force to do everything for you, what will happen if that force happens to be gone one day?

What will you do?

Remember, you have a doer already inside you.

This doesn't mean that you can't have a relationship with somebody who provides a masculine force in your life. On the contrary, if you have this kind of relationship, honor that person. We all have both masculine and feminine forces within us, and we need to respect both elements of ourselves.

I want to convey that it is ultimately a balancing act. Masculine and feminine definitely go together. Be conscious and have gratitude for the masculine and feminine forces in your life.

If you have a man in your life, or someone who strongly represents the masculine in your life—it could be another woman—honor them and give them the approval and the gratitude that they deserve. In addition, honor the masculine within yourself.

There was a period when I was firmly in my masculine energy, a strong woman in my masculine element actively pursuing my goals.

When I started slowing down and understanding myself better, I came to know that I needed to honor the masculine in me, who had taken care of me — in ways I wasn't aware of — and who had helped me become who I was.

Being in the masculine energy is tiring.

Honor that energy so that it understands and knows that it is valued and appreciated. Even if it's not a physical person, it represents the masculine inside you and it is important to honor that.

Give the masculine part of yourself your approval. Honoring it is crucial when you are on the path to the integration of the masculine and feminine.

## Honor Your Feminine Side

On the flip side, if you are a masculine man, you must honor the feminine inside you. You may not be comfortable with feminine energy, and you may resist flowing with this kind of force even though it is an integral part of you.

Allow the force to move through you and honor your feminine energy. This doesn't mean you have to be an effeminate man. It means honoring the place inside of you that is alive with feminine energy.

The feminine is more sensitive, more in flow with nature, and very sensual. It is soft — not weak. Softness doesn't mean weakness; softness is a force, but it is a gentle, guiding, yielding force.

To honor your feminine side, allow yourself to flow with it. Commune with nature and explore your sensitive side.

The key is balance. If you are a super masculine man, you may attract a woman who is overtly feminine and a good complement. You can remind each other to honor the masculine and honor the feminine.

Ideally, your female partner is the most beautiful expression of your feminine inside your physical form.

Honoring that which is the complement to you is valuable in the pursuit of balance in your life.

Now I know it may seem strange, weird, or uncomfortable to admit that you have a feminine and a masculine side. I didn't honor my feminine side very well for much of my life. I am comfortable now, but my comfort comes from a lot of exploration, and trial and error in my own life.

So don't worry too much. Don't get uptight. It's another area of exploration for all of us.

Go deeply into your own wholeness and oneness and become fully aware and comfortable with who you are as a spiritual being on this planet.

## KEEPING THE MASCULINE UNDER CONTROL

For much of my life, my masculine side was out of control. I was not living in balance. The masculine energy drove me for many years and was the reason I had tremendous success in the entertainment industry as an actress, in the stunt industry, and in the training industry. I was a mover and a doer and was always going nonstop.

I was a strong, independent woman, but my life was out of balance.

### If You Don't Access Your Feminine, Your Masculine Will Drive Your Life

Imagine you are on a treadmill, and this treadmill is going at maximum speed all the time. Now imagine this treadmill has been going at maximum speed for about twenty years.

Do you think you might get a little bit tired after that run?

Well, that's exactly what happened to me.

My life got completely out of control. I thought I was doing the right thing by seizing opportunities, going all the time, being constantly on the road, moving, doing, accomplishing, and achieving.

I was burning the candle at both ends, and eventually I was totally exhausted.

If you're not paying attention, and you're following that constant masculine drive, it is definitely going to get out of control. I can tell you this from first-hand experience. Eventually, you will run down roads that are rocky, sharp, and painful.

If you're not conscious of the masculine driving you, it's time to wake up the feminine in order to keep the masculine balanced. There is nothing wrong with using your masculine energy, as it is definitely useful and necessary. However, you can't live in it all the time. This is especially true for women; it creates a state of burnout.

Awaken into the feminine and let the feminine be your guide; let the masculine come out and shine when it is needed.

## Burnout, Stress, and Anxiety

I had heard stories about people burning out and having panic attacks, anxiety, and other stress-related issues. I never thought in a million years that could, or would, be me. I was strong, healthy, and vibrant, but, in December 2012, it all came to a screeching halt.

I found myself in a terrible state—emotionally, physically, and mentally. At one point, I took myself to the emergency room because I thought I was having a heart attack. I had been going nonstop for about two and a half years, working fourteen hours a day.

As I was lying on the hospital bed in the emergency room, the doctor asked me if I was under a lot of stress.

I opened my mouth, and my girlfriend looked at me and said, "Uh, yes."

The doctor told me I wasn't having a heart attack; I was actually having a panic attack from high levels of anxiety.

Right there, that truth smacked me between the eyes with the thing that I never thought would ever happen to me.

I was completely out of balance. Balance is critical. To avoid the path of physical, mental, and emotional exhaustion—balance is absolutely necessary.

I will tell you from first-hand experience that this state was not fun. My recovery was difficult. I had always been active, on-the-go. I ended up not being able to do much of anything—I physically didn't have enough energy to get out of bed. I had let the damage get so far that the recuperation process was extensive and took a long time.

## A Long Recovery: Low Self-Esteem, Lack of Confidence, and Physical Health Issues

This was my darkest hour.

I had no confidence in anything that I was doing. Because my system was so exhausted, even getting out of bed to brush my teeth was a chore. I didn't have the confidence to get in the car and drive safely to the store because I didn't have enough energy.

I didn't feel that I had my wits about me, and my reflexes were slow. I knew that I could not be a safe driver. I couldn't be sure I would see another car in time to avoid hitting it. I didn't know if I could stop for a red light in time.

It was a hard transition period for me. I became a recluse. I rarely left the house. And I cried *a lot*. If I had owned stock in Kleenex, I would have made a decent amount of money during this time.

This is not a fun path. If you are already on it, I would be the first one there to support you through it, not judging, and giving you as much support as possible. But I'd rather help you avoid this path completely. I hope I can give you some insight so you can go down a healthier road.

If you are an over-doer like I was, please remember:

- When you feel the slightest inkling that you're getting ready to run down the road of burnout, immediately take a step back.

- Give yourself breaks regularly, even if you don't feel like you need them. Believe me, you need them.

- Don't judge yourself for taking breaks — do it. You owe it to yourself.

- Whatever you're doing will be there the next day.

- Take time to slow down and relax.

- Be moved by inspiration not desperation.

- Don't get caught in the trap of thinking: *If I don't do it now, I'll miss the opportunity.* It is hardly ever true.

- Keep these words in mind: *Relax. Let go. Trust. Breathe.*

# KEEPING THE MASCULINE AND FEMININE IN BALANCE

## Honor and Acknowledge the Voices of Your Masculine and Feminine

We tend to bury what we don't want to deal with. We tend to hide what we don't want to express. It never, ever works.

That which does not get acknowledged — that which you don't give the opportunity of expression — will work hard to express itself. When it finally does show itself, it often doesn't show up in the most favorable of ways.

Be conscious about honoring any parts of you that you would tend to keep quiet and hidden, including your masculine or feminine energies.

Allowing yourself to be expressive will bring more flow, ease, grace, elegance, and harmony into your entire being and your energetic field.

## Communicate With Your Masculine Energies

When you are out of balance, you need to get in touch with the parts of yourself that are involved. One of the things that I did was actually talk to myself.

I sat down, took a deep breath, let go, got quiet and still. Then, I had an actual conversation with the masculine part of myself.

I said out loud, "Okay, I would like the masculine part to step forward, and I would like to have a conversation."

I proceeded to get curious and asked masculine questions: *How are you feeling? What's going on for you? What's coming up for you?*

A lot of the answers I received when I first had conversations with the masculine were: *I'm tired. I've been working too hard. I'm overwhelmed. I have too much going on.*

Wow! Here was the answer, coming from within.

My masculine side was tired. I needed to give it a break. I needed to slow down and take it easy.

It was in that moment that I could say to my masculine side, "Okay. Awesome. You're going to take a break. We're going to have some downtime."

You need to take care of the different parts of yourself, or you will become unbalanced.

I had to consider:

- *What do I need to feed my masculine?*
- *How do I give it rest?*

- *What's it going to take for me to surrender and let go and not have to be on point all the time?*

Having these kinds of conversations with yourself is valuable. Write down any notes that come up and keep track.

If, like me, you have issues managing your masculine side, this should not be a one-time talk that only takes place when you are having a crisis, but part of an ongoing conversation. You should check in with your masculine once every few weeks, or once a month, whatever feels right to you.

Ask questions.

What does it need to be happy?

What does it need so that it doesn't burn out?

How do you keep it from getting exhausted?

Make it a practice to honor that part of you by talking to it. Make agreements with it and follow through. This is key.

## Make Agreements With Your Masculine Side

Your masculine side is always going to be there. If you start pushing and shoving it down, it will rebel. If you ignore it or push it to the side, it will rise up.

Acknowledge your masculine side, get in touch with it, and take care of it. You want to make agreements with it. You will only be happy and stable when your masculine side is living in harmony and balance with the feminine.

We've been talking about what your masculine needs to be happy.

How can you help it to function in a healthy manner?

One of the things that I decided to do for my masculine was to watch action movies because it makes that part of me feel good. It sounds funny, but it satisfies a masculine need in me to go see some dudes blowing stuff up. I look for action movies that have a lot of movement and a lot of male characters.

Some of the movies that I pick, my feminine likes, too; after all, these are half-naked, hot guys on screen.

Seeing action movies is one agreement that I've made with my masculine.

Make sure that your masculine has the things that it needs. Make those agreements by having conversations from time to time.

How often does it want to go to the movies?

How often does it want to go to the batting cages?

What other masculine activities would it enjoy?

What does it need to stay balanced and feeling strong and powerful?

## Honor the Men in Your Life by Allowing Them to Provide for You

If you're a strong, independent woman, the last thing you are looking for is someone else to provide for you. I always felt that if I let a man provide for me, I owed him. If he took care of something or bought me something, I had to perform for him or have sex with him or do something to compensate for the giving.

This was an unfair assessment. A lot of the men in my life wanted to be there for me and wanted to be allowed to give.

It's a hard practice for me to allow men to do things for me. I have had to make a conscious effort. Even small things were difficult in the beginning.

Do you struggle with allowing men to care for you?

Here are some suggestions:

- Practice allowing men to care for you, even if it feels uncomfortable.

- Ask for small things on purpose, like a glass of water.

- Make yourself sit still and accept assistance sometimes.

- Let go of your pride and realize if a man is trying to help you with something, it doesn't necessarily mean he doesn't think you can't do it yourself.

- Remember to acknowledge and thank men for the care they are providing.

My mentor, Allison Armstrong, says that men often want to provide for women. Any time you feel anxious about owing a man for his assistance, remember that. Allowing a man to provide for you may be a gift to both of you.

For those of us whom are strong, independent women, sometimes we have a hard time attracting a mate into our lives because we don't allow them to provide for us enough.

If you have a man in your life that says he wants to provide dinner for you and wants to fish it out of a river, let him. It may very well be the best fish you've ever had!

# CHAPTER FOUR

# The Force and Flow
# of the Feminine

**EXPRESSING THE POWER OF THE FEMININE**

*Little girls should be seen and not heard.*

Have you heard that expression?

Feminine energy is not always welcome in our society. You may have already realized this.

When you start coming into your own power and your force, your voice comes with it. With that is your expression of what is really going on inside. And not everybody can handle that.

I want to warn you that as you start moving into your own feminine self-expression, there are people whose feathers may get a little ruffled.

Talk about this instead of shoving it under the rug; keep in mind that we can never control what other people think and feel.

Don't be tempted to live your life for the approval of others. Give yourself the gift of allowing yourself to get the skills, tools, and experience of expressing yourself fully, so you feel whole and complete in yourself.

## Don't Be Afraid to Express Yourself

First of all, I want you to face that you are a powerful being. You are a powerful woman. If you're not fully in touch with your power, don't worry! It's going to take practice to become fully self-expressed. The process is tricky and delicate, but the end result will be extremely liberating.

Unless you had a progressive set of parents or peers or a mentor who has allowed you to be fully self-expressed, you probably haven't experienced this kind of expression. It's not something that we are typically taught.

When you are fully self-expressed and speaking the truth, or the truth as you see it, not everyone is going to be able to receive it. I want you to understand that even though not everyone is going to be able to receive it, when you are fully expressed and in your power, it will be freeing for you.

The more skillful you become in your communication, the more freeing it will be. It is deeply satisfying when you are able to express yourself fully.

Don't shelter others from your energy, once you start to feel it. This tendency is understandable; it comes from fear of disapproval and being misunderstood.

However, if you are constantly trying to protect someone else from your full self-expression, they will never truly know who you are. And you will condition people to see you in a way that you may not want to be seen.

## Changing Your Belief System: You're Not Bad

Feeling this feminine energy can be uncomfortable in the beginning. I think I've mentioned this before, and I'm going to say it again: You're not broken. There is nothing wrong with you.

You will need to peel off the layers of the belief system that you've been accustomed to wearing. It's like having ten blankets on when it's cold in the winter. When it's warm in the summer, you will take all those blankets off.

You're not bad.

You're not wrong.

You're not awful for having this power inside of you that wants to come out. It's a natural way of being. It's a natural state of flow. Know that there is nothing wrong with you.

## Developing a Support System That Allows Self-Expression

When you are in the process of opening yourself up to your feminine energy, having a support system is going to be key.

Think about the forces in your life that are supportive and choose to be around them. Bring people into your life who support, love, and care about you, and want to see you at your best.

There are a lot of negative forces out there in the world. There are a lot of people who don't like change. There are people who won't want to move beyond where they are.

Develop a support system of people around you who understand you and will stay with you even when you're not at your best. You might be sad or upset at times. You might be angry. Having a support system of close friends and family will be helpful.

It is best to choose people who understand that you're going through a transition and can be objective and caring at the same time. Don't choose people who will just agree with everything you say; choose people who are good listeners and can be neutral and comforting.

Some people tend to build a shell around themselves when they're going through a tough time. This isn't the best choice. I've had times in my life where I was down and didn't allow a support system to surround me. It only made those periods of my life harder.

One time, lucky for me, some good friends were able to penetrate my shell and tell me they were coming in with me and swimming around in my life. Allowing them in helped bring me to a place of feeling good again. This experience helped me understand the benefit of a support system.

Let people in.

## LIFE CAN BE MESSY, AND THERE'S NOTHING WRONG WITH THAT

Nobody really wants to admit it, but sometimes, life is messy. Sometimes, the feminine is messy. It isn't neat and easy to make sense of. Accept that because you can't change it.

The chaos of life is part of the game. It's part of the flow. It's part of being in a feminine state. It's messy — and that's okay.

### How I Felt When I Was Messy

I was used to being an organized, step-by-step person, a doer. When I felt messy, everything felt like it was falling apart. To me, it felt like a disaster. It was traumatic. I was always the person that everyone else had counted on and relied on to be a rock; it felt awful to be this messy person instead.

It took a lot of courage and acceptance to look at myself and admit I was messy. My life was messy, and that's the way it was going to be for a while.

When you are in the middle of big changes, accept the messiness. Accept what is.

Eventually, you will see that the freedom we gain from messiness is an important part of the process.

## Accepting What Is

It has taken many years for me to accept what is, as opposed to spending all my energy wishing it was some other way. You must surrender — and yes, I mean surrender, a challenging word for strong, independent women, particularly — in order to accept what is.

Accept what is while you are working on understanding yourself.

If it was meant to be some other way, it would be some other way. That's it.

**Finding Clarity**

Finding clarity means to clear your path, to move all the obstacles out of the way. When you can get clarity, then you have somewhere to make a stand and to take a step from.

When you are working on elements of yourself that are beneath the surface, you will have to spend some time gaining an understanding of yourself.

Ask questions. Find out about yourself. Get curious. Find out what is real.

What do you desire?

In my experience, I have come to find there are only a few things people actually desire:

1. We want happiness.
2. We want fulfillment.
3. We want appreciation.
4. We want approval.

These are the four basic human desires that we all have.

When you think of something that you desire, look at this list and analyze your feelings. You may think that what you want is something different, but deep down, it probably is one of these four desires.

Often, our desires are some variation of the fourth item—approval. It is a powerful force. You may not be stepping into your full power because you feel if you step into your full power, then somebody is not going to approve. Somebody is going to be upset.

The first step in finding clarity is to analyze your fears and motivations:

- What are your desires?
- What are your fears?
- Where do your fears come from?
- What is blocking you from your goals?

Sit with yourself to find out what is down deep inside. Find clarity.

Remember the messiness that I was so uncomfortable with?

I eventually found that it was the messiness that helped me find clarity. Allowing life to be messy gives you the freedom to explore everything that it reveals. Out of chaos can come amazing clarity.

Imagine that you have one of those Fabergé eggs, and the only way to see what is inside that egg is to crack it open. You have to let your egg crack, like Humpty Dumpty falling off that wall, so that we are able to see the beautiful yolk inside.

## DESTRUCTION, DISRUPTION, BREAKDOWNS, AND NEW GROWTH

This whole process can be disruptive and destructive. It's going to disrupt your current state of being because you are stepping into new territory.

Our primal brains don't like change; they want our situation to stay the same. There might be a lot of uncomfortable destruction that comes with breaking down old walls and structures. You will be moving through that rubble to find the new growth.

After every destructive occurrence, new growth follows. Know that even though it could be disturbing, and it might disrupt your life or someone else's life, there is a lot of new life that can spring from it.

### Mother Nature's Way

Even though we don't like to hear on the news that a hurricane came through and wiped out a bunch of people or that a forest fire caused mass destruction, this is Mother Nature's way of clearing energy so that something new can arise.

It's hard to understand, but in all parts of life, there are cycles. Mother Nature has her way of cleansing or clearing in order for good things to happen.

Even after a hurricane, people have opportunities to use their gifts to jump to aid others. They put in time, energy, and effort in a way that they never would be able to under other circumstances. There is always a way in which Mother Nature comes through to shake things up so that the new can arise. That's how we learn; that's how we grow.

## Look at Breakdowns as Gifts

What do you do when things go wrong?

One of the biggest challenges I have is dealing with breakdowns, when something doesn't go right, when something is upset. All my life, that's been challenging for me.

When everything has been going great—everything is hunky-dory and feels good—the minute there is a curveball, I feel panicked.

I think: *Oh man, what the hell is this?*

Even now, when I know in my mind that these situations can be turned into something positive, I have to admit that it's still not easy for me.

These situations are opportunities. You have a choice. You can choose to look at it as awful and horrible, or you can take the perspective that it is an opportunity to grow.

## Finding New Perspectives

When something doesn't go the way you planned it, how can you look at it a different perspective?

Imagine yourself standing in front of a mirror. You're looking straight at the mirror. You see yourself from one angle and one angle only. If you don't like the way you look at that angle, you could take a step to the right and turn just a fraction so that you're looking from a different perspective. You might like that angle. That might look better to you. Or maybe you step to the left and look from that angle.

When something happens, change your view of the situation in the same way. Step outside the situation. Imagine yourself taking a step back and looking at it from a broader view, as if you're an eagle looking outside, hovering above, looking around, looking at all sides and taking stock of what really happened.

From the outside, you will see why you feel badly about it, but stepping back will enable you to see the whole picture objectively.

Changing perspective has many benefits:

- You can see the bigger picture.

- You may understand why you feel the way you do.

- You can analyze what led to the breakdown and ask revealing questions.

- You can determine if your behavior was constructive.

- You can see opportunities for growth.

- You can even see benefits of the new situation.

Being able to take a step back to look at the situation from a different perspective, no matter what it is, may not be easy, but it can be beneficial.

Remember, you have a choice. You will always have a choice. You can choose whether to accept what happened or you can resist it. It is a choice. And it's yours.

You can choose to be resentful and angry, or you can change your perspective and see the positive side of an unexpected change in plans.

It is your choice.

This is part of owning your power.

This is part of being who you truly are.

Your soul ultimately knows the goodness of every situation, so allow yourself to really get in touch with your core, your power, and your deepest sense of who you are and who you will be.

# CHAPTER FIVE

# Sustaining Your Power

After you get in touch with your inner power, you will feel the difference.

What do you do next?

We've been talking about discovering, awakening, and gaining access to your power.

Once you do all of that, how do you sustain your power?

What has to happen for that power to stay accessible?

Imagine that you are in your car. Put your foot on the gas pedal and run your car as far as you can for as long as you can until you run out of gas. You have to put more fuel in your car.

Sustaining your power is different from awakening it. In this chapter, we are going to talk about a few of the ways that you can sustain your power.

## REST

As we get busy and productive, using our power to achieve and accomplish our goals, sometimes we forget to take care of our basic essential needs.

You need to stay aware of the needs of your body and mind. I know what it's like when you get on a roll; when exciting things are happening in your life. Before you know it, you're burnt out. We're going to talk about rest because it is a key element in sustaining your power.

### Rest Does Not Mean Sleep

Rest isn't sleep. Sleep is sleep. It's where you're completely out, done, unconscious, in the dream state. Sleeping is not the same as resting.

Resting is much more challenging for most of us.

Resting provides the opportunity to relax your mind, to be in a space where you're not actively thinking about work, errands, or responsibilities.

To rest, you have to give yourself the space to let go of everything — relax, kick your feet up, and get out of production mode.

Rest time allows you to absorb energy. You can restor alone, in nature, or spending quality time with others.

**Finding What Is Restful For You**

What is restful for you?

What activities are restorative for you?

If, after spending time on an activity, you feel both relaxed and energized, you have been restored.

Your answer may be different from mine.

Is it kicking your feet up on the couch and reading a good book that takes you out of production mode?

Or do you need to go outside and sit down by a tree, put your feet on the earth, and get reconnected to nature?

Try some different restful environments and see how you feel. Increase your awareness of the things that nourish and sustain you. Find out what works best to fill you back up after you have been in production mode for a while.

Find what works for you. It's going to be different for everyone.

Explore yourself and have your own adventure in figuring out what helps you rest.

Is it getting into a warm bath with some salts?

Is it watching the sun set?

What helps you to rest and rejuvenate?

## Rest Means That There Is No Production Happening

In our society, we are constantly in production mode. Whether we realize it or not, we are always doing something. For many people, resting will be difficult.

When you sit down to rest, does your mind keep working?

Do your hands search for something to do?

Many people feel guilty unless they are doing something productive. But without rest, you can't replenish your energy supply. When you are in production mode, you are expending energy. When you are resting, you are absorbing energy.

There are times where you need to get out of production mode to rest. I'm sure all of you know this. It isn't a brilliant brainstorm; this is how the cycle of things works. You expend energy, and then you need to rest and regroup. It's vital to have that downtime to recharge, especially for women.

It's like going to the gym and working out. When you do a short burst of speed on a treadmill, there is a point when you will have to stop, to rest and recover.

When you are busy, it might seem like there isn't a moment to rest. At times like these, it's even more important to find downtime. It doesn't need to be long—take ten minutes at a time. Anything can wait for ten minutes, except for actual life-and-death situations, when you would be calling 911.

Find ways to sustain your power. Find moments when you can rest, when you are not actively productive.

## RELAXATION AND REJUVENATION

How easy is it for you to relax?

It has not always been easy for me. Relaxation and rejuvenation are part of the process of successfully owning your power.

### Identify What Feels Relaxing to You

This whole book is about discovering what works for you. It's about getting to know yourself better. It's uncovering the things that work for you.

What is it that relaxes you?

What is it that makes you feel good?

What is it that takes your body from being tense and uptight to being smoothed out, relaxed, feeling in the flow, and supple?

You may have to explore. This is an opportunity for self-awareness, to get to know yourself better. Find the things that work for you.

### Finding Time for Relaxation

What feels good to you?

I love to relax in a few different ways—here are some examples:

- Getting outside and soaking up the sunshine
- Walking barefoot in the sand
- Sitting in a nice, hot tub with lots of bubble bath and Epsom salt
- Doing a jigsaw puzzle
- Taking a sauna, steam, or hot-tub with friends

When you have identified or discovered the things that are relaxing to you, you have to actually do those things. You need to act, to set yourself up to do the things that are relaxing. *You must carve out the time in your schedule to make them happen.*

At the beginning, this won't be hard.

You will think: *This feels good, and I want to do it.*

But then you will get busy again, and your to-do list will start to take priority. At this point, you have to be conscious and aware of the need to set aside time for yourself. Follow through on your promises to your inner self.

Even in the busiest of times, remember those ten minutes. Go outside. Meditate. Do whatever it is that allows you to relax. These opportunities for resting and relaxation are gifts to yourself, and they are vital for your health.

## Implement a Self-Care Routine

Part of cultivating and owning your power is taking care of yourself. Implement a self-care routine for yourself. It doesn't have to be elaborate. It's all about balance: the ebb and the flow, the yin and the yang. It's what helps you stay feeling good.

Find a self-care routine that works for you. Everyone is different.

For you, is it best that you get up in the morning and work out?

Is it good for you to have a nutritional shake every morning?

Do you like cold-pressed juice?

What does your body need?

Find what works for you, and start to put it into practice right away. Implementing a self-care regime or routine keeps your body, mind, and spirit in balance.

For those of you who are used to pouring energy into helping other people, it might feel odd to put energy into taking care of yourself. It may feel strange, weird, or selfish. There is a colleague of mine who says, "You have to be sensibly selfish."

This is absolutely true. When you are sensibly selfish, it gives you the opportunity to take care of yourself, so you have more to give to others. If you're empty and don't have anything to give, you are going to damage yourself trying to give to someone else. I know from experience that this is true.

It may take some practice to start focusing your energy back on yourself, but it is necessary.

## MAINTAINING YOUR BOUNDARIES

Many women have trouble setting boundaries. Some don't have any boundaries whatsoever. We don't want to rock the boat; we don't want to cause problems; we want approval.

This makes it difficult to say *no*.

Setting and keeping clear-cut, distinct boundaries helps you maintain your energy, maintain your power, and maintain your sense of well-being.

You can do all of this in a beautiful, gentle, loving way. Boundaries don't have to be placed in a harsh or angry manner.

It is possible that any new boundaries you set may rock some boats at first with other people, but there is a way in which you can do it that feels good.

Be firm yet kind, and people will come around. You will start cultivating different energy around you, and it will be easier than you think.

## Do You Have a Vampire in Your Life?

In everyone's life, there are forces that drain energy. I call them vampires.

What drains your energy?

Take a moment and reflect on this.

It could be:

- A person
- Your computer
- Your cell phone
- Food
- Alcohol or drugs

Take a good look at yourself and figure out what causes energy to drain out of your life.

Be observant. Identify the vampires in your life.

Is your energy always compromised after a particular activity?

When you spend time with someone, do you always feel drained after you leave them?

If so, there's a good chance they are sucking your energy. These people in your life may not have any idea that they are draining your energy. They are not responsible for fixing this problem; it is up to you to maintain your energetic boundaries.

You may find that there are elements in your life that you need to adjust or remove completely in order to maintain your own sense of well-being.

Nobody should be sacrificing their well-being for anyone else. If you sacrifice your own well-being for someone else, it will deeply affect your health. In addition, you will be angry, resentful, bitter, and unfulfilled.

If you notice that you have a vampire in your life, you need to take the fangs out and stop letting your energy be drained.

## Being Honest With Yourself

You must be observant to find out what your healthiest path is. You must be honest with yourself about what works and what doesn't. This isn't always easy. It can be hard to admit that you need to make changes.

You must be honest enough with yourself to say:

- *These things are not beneficial to me.*
- *These things are draining me of my life force.*
- *These things are working against me.*

It may take a little bit of courage to step up, stand up, and admit you have to make some changes.

If you don't fix the problems in your life, they will continue causing damage. When the pain gets great enough, you will change because you will be forced to.

Remember, there are only two places people move from — inspiration or desperation.

I'd rather see you motivated by inspiration than desperation.

I have come from that place of desperation. Not once, not twice, but many times. The deepest place of desperation came when I was desperate to have my health and wellness back because I had put myself in such a bad position. I had run myself into the ground.

Coming from desperation is no fun. I do not recommend it for anyone, and that means *you*.

Operate from inspiration instead. If you can be inspired to be honest with yourself about the bad things that are happening in your life, then you can change them before you ever approach a state of desperation.

Be curious. Here are some questions to ask yourself:

- *Do I have energy drainers in my life that need to be addressed?*
- *Does my diet need to improve?*
- *Do I need to exercise?*
- *Do I need to stop hanging out with a certain group of people?*
- *Do I have emotional needs that aren't being met?*
- *Do I choose unhealthy ways to meet my needs?*
- *Do I need to take some steps toward becoming balanced?*
- *Do I have trouble being honest and truthful?*

Being honest with yourself is the place to start. It's not always easy, but it's extremely powerful and a key element to owning your power.

**Saying *No, thank you.***

Remember this: *No, thank you* is a complete sentence.

You don't have to follow up with a story, a reason, an excuse, or anything else.

Check in with yourself in any situation, and feel into whether it's right for you.

If not, open your heart to saying *No, thank you.*

Say it with compassion, empathy, and a smile.

It's one of the most powerful things I have learned, and it took me a long time to learn the power of that sentence. Try it for yourself. See how it feels.

Have you been saying *Yes* to a situation because you want approval — because you want to be liked?

If, deep down inside, your answer is *No*, try saying the thing you really feel, which is "No, thank you!"

It's an effective way to:

- Set your boundaries
- Cultivate your energy
- Increase your power

Saying *No, thank you* will actually create an energy in the Universe that brings more respect from other people into your world.

Let's practice this all together: *No, thank you!*

Good job!

If you have no boundaries, you are letting people and their energy run over you. Maintaining your own boundaries helps maintain your energy and your power.

Create your boundaries. Make it a priority. Make boundaries that feel good for you. When you feel good, it's going to reflect in the world around you.

# *Conclusion*

Congratulations!

In reading this book, you've taken the time to:

- Learn more about yourself
- Understand yourself better
- Be proactive
- Uncover the power that is within you
- Learn how to cultivate, increase, and sustain that power

This is only the beginning of your journey.

It's all a process. You are a different person today than you were yesterday. Every single moment of the day, your cells are changing and growing. You are changing, and you are growing.

It may take a while for your mindset to catch up to the things that you really want for your body, spirit, your soul, and your self. You may not have understood or agreed with everything in this book; there may have been parts of the process that you were not ready to hear.

I'm going to remind you right now to be gentle with yourself. Don't get too caught up in how much you did or didn't do. Any little thing that you have done is a step. If you're anything like me and are used to taking ten steps at a time, this may be hard for you to accept. Always remember that you are growing. Don't forget to acknowledge your efforts and pat yourself on the back sometimes. Be gentle with yourself.

The feminine is not always gentle. We see this when Mother Nature comes through and does her thing in the form of hurricanes and storms. Sometimes, though, it is the gentlest force that can cause the biggest shifts.

If you have a personal storm happening in your life, there is always a calm before the storm and a calm after the storm. Be willing and open to be in the storm. Create the kind of energy in your life that puts you in the eye of the storm.

Yes, there are going to be times where you will be the whipping wind. There are other times where you are going to be the light drizzle. Other times, you will definitely be the torrential downpour. But be gentle with yourself. All of these things are part of you. Allow them to be. It's part of your power. It's part of who you are as a woman.

Continue to explore. Be open. Be curious. Read. See what resonates with you. Visit our website to find more resources — you will find contact information in the *Next Steps* section of this book.

Understand that embracing the feminine takes time. If you have lived in a masculine world and have been caught up in a fast-paced life, you will need time to adjust. Be gentle and move gradually. Keep reminding yourself to be gentle with yourself. One step at a time.

Resting and rejuvenation are necessary for survival and for gaining and sustaining power. Nurture yourself. Take care of yourself.

There is no way you can take care of anyone else if you don't take care of yourself. If your life is based on helping other people, taking care of other people, and serving other people, that is wonderful. We're all really here to serve; we all have gifts; and we have amazing love to shine.

Remember, the only way to really help anyone else to shine their light is to shine yours as well. But it is hard to shine your light if you are exhausted and burnt out.

So be kind to yourself. Love yourself. Honor yourself. Empower yourself. And give yourself the opportunity to slow down, take a breath, and cultivate your power, so you can go out and shine it to the rest of the world.

To your power, your light, and your freedom.

# *Next Steps*

Please visit the Power of the Goddess Website for our upcoming programs and a list of resources to guide you on your path.

Use Promo Code: POG$250 to take $250 us dollars off of any "Power Of The Goddess" or "Women of Power" Program or Retreat over $1,595 usd

Use Promo Code: POG$100 to take $100 dollars off of any "Power Of The Goddess" or "Women of Power" Program or Retreat priced between $595 and $1,495 usd.

**Follow us!**

**Website**:    powerofthegoddess.com
           www.womenofpower.us

**Instagram**: @powerofthegoddess

**Twitter**:     @PwrOfTheGoddess

**Facebook**:  PowerOfTheGoddess AND
            Marjeanholdenfans

**Twitter**:     @marjeanholden

**Periscope**: @marjeanholden

# Additional Endorsements

"For all the would-be superwomen out there who are exhausted, depleted, and uninspired, Marjean's straight-up wisdom will feel like a fresh spring rain. Pulling back the curtain on the what it really means to be in our feminine—and offering practical advice for incorporating that life-giving energy into a busy modern lifestyle—she gently guides each of us back to the goddess within."

– Kelly Notaras, Writer, Editor, Speaker and Founder of kn literary arts

"I've known Marjean for over ten years and she is a strong and sensitive woman with a great presence. Her book, *The Power of the Goddess*, will enhance people's journeys (both women and men) right away and long term."

– Dr. Brian Alman, Author of *The Inner Voice*, *Mind-Body Weight Loss*, *Less Stress for Kids* and Founder of TruSage

"It doesn't surprise me that this book is written in such a personal way and with a depth of insight that will no doubt touch the deepest emotions and soul of every reader. If I had my way, this book would be compulsory, gifted to every young woman as she enters that inescapable vastness that will inevitably confront her: womanhood. This book invites exploration of what the best kind of woman would be for every one of the gentle yet powerful gender, and equally, it provides the warm, sure hand of a guide who has experienced rough seas that same vast ocean called womanhood can bring. I encourage you to enter this book with your vulnerability in hand, and the knowledge that alongside vulnerability comes true power, or as it is otherwise referred to, *empowerment*—for the nature of all life and being-ness is of duality. With the day comes night, alongside the cold comes warmth, and through darkness shines a beacon of light. I invite you to take this wonderful journey with the equally wonderful Marjean. And If you are a man, then within the pages of this book you will find a refreshing new way to see the beauty of the women in your life and with that a new way to honor them, and ultimately deepen your relationships in a more meaningful way. I hold the intention that this book will find its way into the hands of young ladies across the world as they flourish into all they can be as women. Marjean I love your gift to the world, and I honor you."

– Kurly Marwaha, Master Feng Shui and
Energetics Practitioner

"As a man reading this book I'm deeply yet softly invigorated to my core by Marjean's intimate journey to accepting the divine goddess within herself, feminine and masculine in its total balance and application to everyday life. As a man, it affirms me to know that our true women are making their epic journey back home to themselves. Full heart, full healing power, full voice, and full expression into a world that has been needing the true woman to remind us all of our divinity. Thank you, Marjean. You've shared parts of yourself that leave me no choice but to love, appreciate and respect you and all women in my life exponentially more. I thank you on behalf of all men for helping our women heal and come back home."

> – K.J. Ellsworth, Emmy-Award Winning Film
> and Television Actor

"I first met Marjean at an event I attended in 2008. She was on stage, in front of over 800 people. As I entered from the back of the room, her Goddess Energy was evident! I reached out and shared what I experienced and she had this smile that is piercing to the soul and said, 'Thank you!' I have been blessed to share the stage with Marjean along this journey and have the utmost deserved respect for her. As I was reading *The Power of the Goddess*, I was blown away by my male thoughts regarding what many females have to overcome in this stereotypical world. Marjean overcame her life struggles and within, found her inspiration as well as courage, strength, and the will to be more, do more, and share more. As a result of reading this book, my life has transformed in a miraculous way. I believe *The Power of the Goddess* book will do the same for you! As you read this amazing book you have in your hands, you realize Marjean is the *real deal* and is walking her talk! You will benefit from her insights, wisdom, and inspiration that she has gathered over the years, which she now shares with you in this book. Buckle up and enjoy!"

– Ruben Mata, Speaker, Trainer, Author, U.S. World Peace Ambassador

"This book will help you find the power within you so that you can shine it out to the world."

– Keith Leon, Multiple Bestselling Author, Speaker and Book Publisher

# About the Author

ACTRESS and STUNTWOMAN
TRANSFORMATIONAL TRAINER
MOM

*I am here to touch, move, and inspire others
to live in their purpose with power and passion.*

Standing nearly six feet tall, Marjean Holden is not classified as the typical girl next door. With a wide range of abilities, she has been an exceptional commodity in the entertainment industry. Springing from a family of entertainers, she knew at a young age that *The Biz* was definitely her thing. She started her quest in the fourth grade where she produced, directed, and starred in her first stage play.

After making her professional acting debut in the feature film *Bill and Ted's Excellent Adventure*, she moved to Los Angeles and worked consistently in the field for more than twenty years. Her early credits include a role in Universal's *Stop! Or My Mom Will Shoot*, with Sylvester Stallone, starring roles in Imperial Entertainment's *Ballistic* with Richard Roundtree and Michael Jai White, and *The Philadelphia Experiment II* with Brad Johnson, where she replaced Courtney Cox, and popular television shows like *The Fresh Prince of BelAir*, *JAG*, HBO'S *Tales from the Crypt*, *Star Trek: Deep Space 9*, *La Femme Nikita*, *Suddenly Susan*, and *The Steve Harvey Show*.

Marjean was featured in Steven Spielberg's *The Lost World* and Jan De Bont's *Speed 2: Cruise Control*. Marjean also starred as Sheeva, the four-armed fighting machine in New Line Cinema's box office hit *Mortal Kombat: Annihilation*, and was one of John Carpenter's master vampires in *Vampires*. Marjean portrayed series regular *Dr. Sarah Chambers* in the series *Crusade*, written by award-winning writer and producer J. Michael Strazynski, and starred as Lt. Joyce Darwin in Paramount Pictures' *Code Red: The Rubicon Conspiracy*, both of which re-air regularly on the Syfy Channel. Marjean also appeared in Disney's *George of the Jungle 2*, where she played the role of Sally, a henchwoman hired to steal the deed to Ape Mountain. In 2005,

Marjean played the role of Officer Carol Flores, dying in the arms of Bruce Willis in the action film *Hostage*.

In addition to working in the film industry, one of her other passions had always been to transform the lives of others. In 2003, she attended a seminar given by a personal development company called *Peak Potentials*. She went from student to employee to trainer in only eighteen months and became their first female trainer, leading T. Harv Eker's world-renowned *Enlightened Warrior Training Camp* in 2006. After taking a year and a half off to raise her daughter in 2007, she rejoined the training team at *Peak Potentials*. In 2008, when the company expanded, she started leading the program overseas with *Success Resources*. She has now transformed and inspired tens of thousands of students by leading T. Harv Eker signature courses in Malaysia, Singapore, the United Kingdom, Germany, Holland, Italy, Taiwan, Spain, Japan, Canada, Brazil, and Australia. Marjean put her film career on hold for a few years to solidify her place in the personal-growth world, however, she is now back in the industry, playing herself in the upcoming release *Bring Me the Head of Lance Henriksen*, from award-winning writer, director, and producer, Michael Worth. She is currently in preparation for the upcoming Gena8 Productions film, *Garrison 7*, where she will be playing the role of the Empress Morgana.

In addition to her film history, she is a certified *Sacred Gifts Guide* and a certified *Orgasmic Meditation Trainer and Coach*. In 2016, she launched *Three Source Enterprises* with two other veterans in the personal-growth industry. This new training company will focus on three key functions: Event Production, Coaching/ Mentoring, and Consulting. She is the Owner and President of *Power of the Goddess*, which focuses on the empowerment of women through highly experiential retreats, live events, online products, and resources.

Above all, Marjean loves helping others break through their limiting beliefs to achieve higher levels of fulfillment, joy, prosperity, and success.

Manufactured by Amazon.com
Columbia, SC
08 April 2017